T0195967

Adam's
Book of Poetry
Living Life Like a Boss

TINA HASSAN

Archway Publishing books may be ordered through booksellers or by contacting:

Archway Publishing
1663 Liberty Drive
Bloomington, IN 47403
www.archwaypublishing.com
1 (888) 242-5904

Because of the dynamic nature of the Internet, any web addresses or links contained in this book may have changed since publication and may no longer be valid. The views expressed in this work are solely those of the author and do not necessarily reflect the views of the publisher, and the publisher hereby disclaims any responsibility for them.

Any people depicted in stock imagery provided by Getty Images are models, and such images are being used for illustrative purposes only.
Certain stock imagery © Getty Images.

ISBN: 978-1-4808-9282-8 (sc)
ISBN: 978-1-4808-9283-5 (e)

Print information available on the last page.

Archway Publishing rev. date: 7/13/2020

*"To My Loving Son, Adam,
Forever in My Heart"*

~My Pride & Joy~

Adam, you are my loving child.
The small things you do makes me so proud of you!
I only hope one day you will not grow up to be too wild.
You took away all my blues.

Since the day you were born,
You brought joy to my heart.
You are my sweet little boy,
And it all began from the very start.
So, until the end, you will always be my pride and joy.

~Adam's 6th Birthday~

It's Adam's 6th birthday,
Hoping for a guitar, he dearly did pray,
Adam wished for a fun day, before he dozed off to sleep,
Hoping he wouldn't get anything so cheap.
Adam woke up not being able to sleep,
He came down without making a peep,
He was too excited,
And up he went back to his room
and turned out the lights.
The next morning, he awoke saying:
"Mommy! Mommy! It's my birthday!"
I told him to get ready for his big day,
Off to Chuck E Cheese we went, Which,
turned out to be a fun day,

Adam's got everything he's wished
for and even more, I must say.
Money, toys, clothes, and even his shiny new red guitar,
There it did lie on the side of the salad bar,
Adam stared at me and he couldn't believe his eyes,
Jeez Adam, you know it's a sin to spy.

Next day we went back to Chuck E
Cheese' since we had more tokens,

The prizes he's won had him going on talking,
Later we went to play basketball one on one,
Adam has beaten me eleven to one.

~The Flying Kite~

Adam and mommy went to the park,
When he arrived, he has seen other kids flying their kite.
"Let's kick the sparkling ball around" says: Adam's
mommy, *"we can see the colorful sparks?"*
Adam says: *"not today mommy, today
I just want to fly a kite."*
"Ok" says: mommy, *"we can go to
the store and buy you a kite."*
Adam was excited and on his way to
the store he picked up two sticks,
And in his pocket he had a handkerchief that was white.
He found a rubber band on the floor and
pulled off a string from his shirt.

"Mommy I have an idea" said: Adam. "I want to make my own kite instead of buying one." "I can put the two sticks together to make an X," "And tie the rubber band around them with my handkerchief; thanks to the wind I won't even have to run." "Oh Adam, I'm so proud of you, mommy just wants to give you lots of hugs and kisses," said: mommy.
"Mommy look I even have a string from my shirt," said: Adam.

"So even if I did run and fall, you wouldn't care if my clothes were filled with dirt, because you would say: "It's ok Adam, we can always wash clothes even if covered in dirt."

~Ties! Ties!! & More Ties Everywhere!!!~

Colorful ties,

Polka dot ties,

Stripe ties,

Wow even square ties,

Circle ties,

Triangle ties!

Bow ties,

Suit ties,

And even birthday ties,

Ties, Ties, & More Ties Everywhere!

Can you guess what kind of tie I am wearing?

~My Mommy~

My mommy cuddles with me,
Kisses me,
Hugs me,
And is always proud of me.

My mommy washes my clothes,
Tickles my toes,
Giggles with me,
And plays with me.

My mommy takes me for a walk,
And we always have a good talk,
She sings to me,
And gives me lots of bubble baths.

My mommy is the best,
She says it's time for a good night's rest,
She reads me a bedtime story and kisses my forehead,
My mommy says sweet dreams my precious
angel and tucks me into bed.

My mommy belongs to me,
As you can see,
I am glad she's my mommy,
I love you mommy!

Let's play:

I like to play with my trains on rainy days.
What do you like to do on rainy days?

Eating healthy keeps me strong. Can
you help me find an apple?

A delightful collection of simple verse and photographs that celebrate a little boy's everyday experiences through the eyes of his mother.

Tina Hassan - Receives Music Award

Tina sings to her fountain of joy, Adam, since he was born. In addition, she takes his photos and attaches them to complete this book.

 "Author Tina Hassan enjoys spending much quality time with her son, Adam. She began publishing her writings in 2013. When she's not writing, she's on the road traveling or cooking & baking up a storm in the kitchen. When she was 9 months old she was chosen as front cover magazine in the Hollywood Spotlite. In 2016, Tina walked the red carpet in Atlanta, Georgia with her son, Adam, with other great authors. Author Tina Hassan has been on national television for her photography at Kiddie Kandids in 2007. She enjoyed coaching youth soccer at the YMCA in Paterson, NJ in 2008; she played soccer in high school, her position was defense. She was also in the choir where she received an award. Author Tina Hassan holds a bachelor's degree in English Major from Montclair State University & Associates degree in Humanities/Liberal Arts from Passaic County Community College."

Printed in the United States
By Bookmasters